RECOVERY

Through

POETRY

Bernadette Kirwan

First Published in Australia in 2023 by Bernadette Kirwan.

Copyright © Bernadette Kirwan 2023

Bernadette Kirwan has asserted her moral right to be identified as
the author of this work.

Printed through Kindle Direct Publishing.

Hardback ISBN 978-0-6459520-0-1
Paperback ISBN 978-0-6459520-1-8

ABOUT THE AUTHOR

Bernadette is both a teacher and a multiplatform content creator.

As a survivor of child abuse, she seeks to empower other survivors on their journey to recovery. She also has a passion for educating and entertaining the world about her Irish and Palestinian heritage, by introducing everyone to their rich and vast cultures.

Her overall goal with both writing and content creation is to be a part of the voice that creates awareness and fosters change around the topic of child abuse and cultural diversity.

For more of her content, please visit:

Website bernadette-kirwan.com
Instagram @bernadette.kirwan
Facebook @Bernadette Kirwan
YouTube @bernadette.kirwan
TikTok @bernadette.kirwan

ACKNOWLEDGEMENTS

To the people who helped bring this all to life, that made this book at all possible...

~ Illustrator, Ismail Youssef
You were the first person to jump on board, offering to help me with so many drawings. You were so kind and patient with me when it came to your time and I am incredibly grateful to have had someone who could so easily bring my ideas to life, despite only having my words to work with. A brilliant artist to say the least. Thank you.

~ Editor, Phillip Massaad
I grew up in admiration of your intelligence and it has been so humbling to have now sat beside you whilst you fine-tuned my ideas, in the most holistic of literary ways. Thank you for your wisdom and the countless times you offered your advice so willingly. You're honestly like the big brother I never had. Thank you.

~ Book Designer, Moses Hosni
The man of the hour, the one who gave up so many nights to not only learn but then also successfully design the entire layout of my book. For having so much faith in me, for believing in my message and for being my backbone in all of this, thank you. You're the best friend everyone needs, the one who makes your life so much more bearable. Thank you.

DEDICATION

For Noel and Martha Kirwan,
or as they are more affectionately known,
Granny and Grandad.

I owe you both my life. From its conception, through to its continuation, I only exist today thanks to you both. I only lead the life I do today thanks to you both. None of this would have been possible without your collective generosity and I can only hope, that in whatever small way I attempt to "return the favour", so to speak, I do so in the currency of pride. I hope I've made you both proud. All my writing only exists, thanks to the journey you have helped me navigate in healing and thanks to the environment you have fostered in simply my being. If there ends up being anyone out there who appreciates reading my work, their appreciation will be owed to you and not me.

The house that sheltered my pen, the bed that rested my mind, the light that witnessed my first few lines and the sustenance that fed my never-ending rhymes, all of it came from you; my beautiful, selfless and utterly devoted grandparents. Everything came through your hearts, into my soul and onto my paper. It is an honour to publish this body of work in dedication to you both and also in the last name I inherited from our wonderful family. I hope you love it as much as I love you both. Granny, my role model, Grandad, my hero – together you're the greatest blessing I have and will ever know.

Go raibh míle maith agat[1]

---

[1]An Irish saying meaning "may you have a thousand good things" or similarly "a thousand thank yous".

welcome one and all,

to a collection of poetry written from the heart

or maybe from my mind, a place i never thought smart

yet somehow i hear things – is it peace to my cause

as if proof that we're the creator of our own applause

welcome to a recovery through poetry,

Berna xxx

CONTENTS

PART ONE

ABUSE

acts of evil committed against mankind;
where one is wrongly used, taken advantage of in time
and when one is a child there is no greater crime

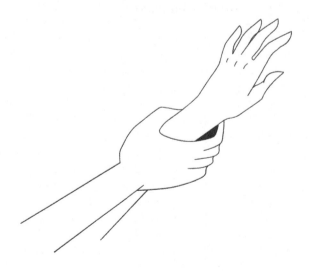

sometimes your childhood

steals from your adulthood

sincerely,

an abused child

POETIC JUSTICE

i'm using poetic justice
to solve what i entrusted

in the woman i called mother
but instead wished i was some other

type of unborn being
she would have made me too if grandad hadn't stopped her seeing

see she didn't want a daughter
because she wasn't mentally ready for the order

that life would provide
the day i did arrive

i hope one day though she will understand
at least to the degree i had to withstand

how her neglect nearly ruined me
but thankfully it grew in me

poetic justice in a mind full of rhymes
because what she stole from me is time

and now i'm taking back what's mine
the health of my mind

DEAR MUM

dear mum, my machiavellian
cunning, subjective and oh so deceptive
in this life you've been utterly inventive

especially with me, your daughter of hate
drowning in desire to please you so great

instead of bathing me in a life of love and knowledge
all i felt and learnt was a life of pain and stoppage

stopping me from thinking and feeling
if it was in any way different from how you were reeling

because a child in their own mind is a child without ties
and you couldn't have that in your house of lies

like marie antionette[2], full of so much reign
your cake was served on a platter drowning in pain

you failed me like you failed yourself
but i promise you i'll learn how to take care of myself

lying about your own unvalidated self-worth
as if the only way to sooth your unsung song since birth

it is not my fault you live a life you hate
yet you blame me as if that will help you elate

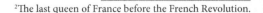

[2]The last queen of France before the French Revolution.

14

see what you forget is that i am from you
mother and daughter, that you cannot argue

and so in you lies the seed
of a starved unwanted weed

one you plucked dry
only to send out without even one try

despite having no wings
because you clipped them in my very first spring

i had to learn how to walk without holding on to your hands
because trust was not served in your pillar of demands

but now i run free from your rugged terrain
because i realised i had so much to regain

a life worth living
even if my own mother wasn't so forgiving

why, some may ask
the question is in the task

to live and let live
because no matter how little they give

that doesn't define your story
you can create all your own glory

life is the ask
please give it your best mask

until the day comes along
where you proudly sing your own song

bare your own face
on a stage beaming with grace

while you smile without vengeance
because there's beauty in your subtle transcendence

and besides, how were you to even know
when you were given so little room to grow

but the main thing is you're here now
so please do not back down now

dear mum, this is for you
you always told me i was tone deaf but that just wasn't true

you just didn't want to listen
instead, you floated in and around that prison

but i broke free
can you believe it, me

and i'll never return
no matter how hard the burn

because every moment is worth it
even the ones where i realise i am not perfect

so thank you, yes thank you
for being my biggest inspiration i'll argue

because you inadvertently taught me what not to be
and how to live a life for me

because growing up all alone
when your mother is too busy on her self-appointed throne

is a lesson for the unheard
that when heard become their own bird

free at last
to leave this broken life in the past

dear mum, i forgive you
it took me a while but i too relieve you

of your role as my mother
because as your daughter all i did was suffer

you know it's like those that kept telling me to
forgiveness is for me and not you

as hard as it was, i have now forgiven you
but i'll never be able to forget all that you put me through

dear mum, i loved you, not sure you knew that
but thank you and goodbye; i'm never coming back

ELEVEN

i was just eleven
a young girl never dreaming of sending myself to heaven
until that morning when you came in at seven

confused, full of lies, i could only wonder why
a grown man would jump inside and say to me let's try
because who knows what could happen if you start to pry

reflect on the pain you bore me
as you laid there and mentally tore me
ready to be the creation of what just might contort me

a moment in time
of which i will never forget your crime
where you used and abused until you no longer did whine

took my clothes off and told me it's ok
confused without a real father, all i could do was pray
and hope that one day you would no longer want to play

treating me like your own unloved toy
as if i were your doll that need not deploy
into a normal life, without all of my joy

fast forward to year nine
and suddenly heaven seems so fine
because your crime has now become my untold 'whine'

but my faith keeps me here
with eyes drowning in tears
i'd do it if it weren't for the overwhelming fear

i'm no longer eleven though and now years have passed
but lo and behold, it still has yet to be your last
because each morning with you brings another new pass

you smile at me as if i'm your wife
meanwhile you're ruining my entire life
when will you learn that you were the source behind my knife

oh, that's right, when i'm twenty-two
and not because you're finally through
but because i ran away and now i'm nowhere for you to do

you ruined a little girl full of hopes and dreams
who left and now must sew the patches in her life full of seams
because you ripped and filled my soul with nothing but internal screams

my life is not over though, i'll make sure i'm free
what you weren't counting on is how strong an eleven year old could be
and so here i rise after years of fighting for little and old me

SEX

there's just something so horrible to me about the topic of sex
almost like, for some, that one abominable ex

the one that no one ever wants talk about
and that's how i feel about this topic, i could go without

i'm not sure if it's because there's something wrong with me
or if my childhood had anything to do with the robbery

some think it's a miracle i'm thirty-one and never pregnant
but actually, it would be a miracle if i ever got pregnant

someone once told me that girls who were abused growing up
end up addicted as they get older, as if sobering up

so why did i go the opposite way
i feel guilty for it, please someone say

that this is just another normal trauma response
to handling how someone mishandled you; it's a nuisance

but i have to remember that it's not my fault
despite him trying to manipulate me into thinking it was, like a cult

i do pray though, that one day i'll look forward to it
however, i can't help at the moment but cower to it

B.K

the idea; it's a topic that's always there
if not in relationships, it's in movies, music, everywhere

and i just turn a blind eye
not sure if that's the wrong thing to do or why

i can't seem to disassociate
this topic from him, it irritates

me in every way
because despite having grown up and run away

it's like he still has access to my emotions
because he's still ruining my motions

with anyone that i meet
how do i move past this antagonising leech

it has been nine years
and the idea still fills with me tears

but one day i'll gain that part of me back
i've been working so hard getting everything else on track

so perhaps more time is all i need
accompanied by the right guy who will understand my plead

B.K

love is no friend of mine

every time someone reaches out - decline

sincerely,

daddy issues

NO RHYME OR REASON

there's no rhyme or reason
that is fit for the season

when it comes to a parent's doubts
which then makes a child go without

for so long children have been taught
to keep their mouths shut, even when distraught

and yes, i do believe in much respect
but never when you put one in distress

mum, are you listening
i've finally stopped whispering

i've so many unanswered questions
but let's start with your intentions

why turn two into three
if you never wanted me

there's such a thing as protection
it's best used if you're not going to pay attention

if you couldn't raise me to at the very least be happy
you should have handed me to someone who would have been happy

24

to raise me with love like my father wanted
but you couldn't have that, him get what he wanted

so instead, you kept me locked up in your house
so you could treat me like some sort of mouse

running around doing all your work
instead of playing dolls, i was playing housework

while you took the credit for all of my achievements
despite the pain evident in my bereavement

with every passing year
was it not obvious i couldn't hear

how you were manipulating my mind
into thinking you were one of a kind

until dad came back
and gave me a "smack"

"back to reality"
like eminem said, "there goes gravity"[3]

because suddenly i'm no longer falling
every time you come calling

you say you're my mother but that's just a title
for which to be worthy you can't act so entitled

---

[3]Lyrics from the song *Lose Yourself* by Eminem, an American rap artist.

25

do you regret all the pain you caused in my youth
for without i could have gone and it wouldn't have cost me my truth

instead, now i'm all wrapped up
feeling like one big overfilled cup

hiding my true self from the world
i'm not lying i'm just not giving all of me to the world

instead, i've internalised
so much that could have been personalised

you knew that life would already be hard enough
but you couldn't help yourself, you just had to be 'tough'

and now i'm still learning how to undo all the narcissistic things you
taught me
life has been a great teacher though, when it comes to rewriting how you
fought me

as if i was some sort of enemy
i mean they do say you can create your own cemetery

but rather than dig your own grave with time and love
you tried to hurry mine along with wine and shove

me to one side as if i wasn't even from you
but unfortunately i must be, at least of you

because sometimes what i see in the mirror
is a reflection of who should have been my pillar

moving on though, on this fine bit of paper
i want to remind you all that it is better to be safer

more than sorry, which i should see in my mother's eyes
she might not have taught me much but what she omitted did in entice

a life of rewriting, in therapy for my nurture
so moving forward i can learn from her mistakes - bullet proof my future

and that doesn't mean children like us have become ideal
just because right now we may currently appeal

to our younger self, crying
who would have given anything to be climbing

the ladder we've now found
and created, built up from the ground

no not ideal
just perfectly real

because unlike 'mummy'
who thought of herself as if honey

i have learnt life isn't meant to be narcissistic
and definitely not so pessimistic

no realistic and beautiful
the way nature intended, bountiful

the main life lesson she was missing
was one of life's true blessings

humility
unavailability

how - first, ground yourself
and then second, remove thyself

recover from all your past pain
but don't replace them with new people in vain

instead, learn to like your own company
so then you'll find freedom and not have to accompany

anyone and everyone, in order to feel alive
because there's no rhyme or reason in living just to survive

B.K

RUNAWAY

let the chase begin
i'm going to make up for time that was stolen from within

i guess i have so much to say on this topic
after all, it was years in the making getting ready to leave this tropic

this heat, drowning in my flooding sweat
because i work double time, filling with regret

well actually, it was a decision made over night
but the pain and sadness had been brewing in plain sight

anxious with questions
unsure of my intentions

because whilst i know i'm dying
my 'mother' makes me feel like i'm not trying

hard enough to earn my keep
despite all the hard work, knee deep

i'm this family's cleaner, server and all-round worker
anything but what i should be, a loved and happy daughter

so i'm running outside and also within
to make up for lost time with my own kin

i can and i have forgiven her for almost everything
but it's hard to forget the time taken from the very thing

that i bonded with the most
from the beginning with my host

until she abandoned her vows
running off to that paedophile clown

as if he even compares
to my father's family of heirs

inheriting love and kindness
two things both timeless

but i guess they both know nothing about that
because i never saw a day where either would provide that

lost, perhaps falling behind a mountain
pretending he's the sun and she his fountain

of what, definitely not joy
i saw that night when he was choking her like a toy

his cousin begging
and her just letting

so harsh and aggressive with me
and yet allowing this creep to walk free

30

how was that normal
i was seven and all she could do was act cordial

pretending that everything would be normal one day soon
as if his hands around her oxygen supply shouldn't have been the moon

that rose over the last night she ever let him dream
of a life with her, influencing me - couldn't she read

between the lines on what that would teach me
thank god i already had a dad that beseeched me

to never give in
to open up my eyes and begin

the absolute greatest chase
and to never waste

what he knows is inside me
true irish and palestinian heresy

that ironically
is never impropriety

i'm a stranger in my own home
because my 'mother' makes me feel like i'm all alone

which is why i must run away
because growing up here feels like i'm a stray

B.K

TWENTY - TWO

it's july 22nd, 2014
and i live a life my mother often demeans

i'm twenty-two years old
and my soul is growing cold

tired of living this life
slowly turning me strife

but i'm about to do the hardest thing i could ever imagine
something for myself, rather than waiting to see what will happen

it's not often one gets a chance to restart
but i'm about to run away and silently depart

it's 6am and i've made my mother her tea
i hand it to her in bed and tell her i'll back after three

only i won't be back, not this time anyway
i know i've tried this before but this time i can't stay

goodbye to my brother and my sweet sisters too
i'm sorry but i promise i'm just broken and trying to pull through

i want to be back but this time on my own terms
i'm just not sure how or when, i guess we will learn

32

a kiss on the cheek as i wave bye through my tears
i hope to see you again one day, hopefully it won't be years

turn around, walk down that concrete path
don't look back now, you'll only face her wrath

take the corner, there's the bus waiting
ready to be the start of a journey engraving

memories in my mind as each second passes by
i'm off to find a new home, i just don't know why

perhaps it's because subconsciously i've finally learnt
that wanting to be happy is not a crime and can be earnt

or maybe it's for my childhood friend
a friendship with a guy i can't fathom might end

if i stay here any longer
because mother realised he opened my eyes to wonder

whether it's for he or i
it doesn't matter as long as i try

it's time to do myself a favour
and run away from my mother's forced harsh labour

the bus travels off
i arrive to university aloft

33

B.K

then head off to class
i present my assessment task

now it's time to send my mother my goodbye
in an email i'm typing, fingers shaking as i try

my classmate jay is sitting next to me
assuring me of what will be

press send on an email of cessation
because this business is no longer in operation

block, delete
no more repeat

of all her misuse
and of his abuse

dad has me now
it's time to ride over the harbour bridge and say ciao[4]

before i'm finally home
to a real family i can call my own

granny and grandad too
plus a sister, to name a few

then we all went off to dinner
i ordered the fish feeling like a sinner

[4]An informal Italian salutation used to express both "hello" and/or "bye".

afraid she'd find me because she somehow knew
that she'd kidnap me, taking me back blue

but that was all just the trauma learnt
something i'd have to heal from no matter how it hurt

now it's time to go back to my new home
learn how to put the kettle on, together not alone

grandad made me a cup of tea
up until then, no one had ever done that for me

something that may seem so trivial
and yet now is something for me so serial

we talked for hours and then days
upon reflection i'm so amazed

how i was gone for so long
but it was as if time had got it all wrong

like i'd never left and better yet
suddenly i no longer regret

safe, out of harm's way
there's no step-dad coming in to play

nor mum pulling me by my ear
screaming at me, creating fear

35

B.K

no, not this time, not anymore
now i can finally sleep some more

i'll have a few nightmares for a while
apparently they'll go when i'm no longer in denial

when i go and seek help
speak my truth and not yelp

and in time i'll find my wings
learn how to truly soar each spring

the nightmares only come once every blue moon now
but at least i've learnt how to see the beauty in what it endows

i wake each morning and relearn how to befriend gratitude
oh, how it truly helped me alter me entire attitude

to life which i've learnt can be heaven on earth
but not at first, from the beginning of your birth

rather eventually as you grow
and take care of the seeds you sow

like flowers, one day you'll bloom and all
but not just in summer, also in fall

i'm no longer twenty-two
and sometimes i wish i foreknew

but then again i've learnt to like myself
better yet, love myself

and i couldn't be me
without all that, i guarantee

so moving forward
because we are not corded

i'm no longer growing cold
but instead, simply old

and the beauty of that is in the lessons i've learnt
and hopefully can share with anyone who has been hurt

i know life can be hard
believe me, sometimes i wanted to part

but this world needs you here
it wouldn't be the same if it were missing you near

this is your life, no one else can live it
whether you're happy or sad, believe it

whether you're twenty-two, unsure of where to go
or home but homeless because your soul has no room to grow

life always has a means of working itself out
so remain ready to live, even when in doubt

you'll find sooner or later
the answers come like pen to paper

even if you're sixty, waiting to run free
it's better to sting now even if you run the risk like a bee

it's so true when they say
the grass isn't greener over the way

it's greener where you water it
as long as you look after it

by "it" i mean you
i cannot express this to be more true

after everything, you still care for everyone else
and yet never stop and think of just yourself

pretty soon you'll have nothing left to give
if you don't stop and learn how to simply live

now i'm thirty-one
and the fun has just begun

i've finally learnt a thing or two
since that day when i was just twenty-two

grateful is an understatement of how i should feel
and don't get me wrong i do but i still can't believe this is real

B.K

so thank you to my family, the kirwan[5] clan
you're my first real supporters and i'm your number one fan

thank you for taking me in at a time where i felt dead
you resurrected my soul and put my pain to bed

it wakes up every now and again
and you're always there to remove any chain

but these chains have also taught me what true family is for
and i'll make sure the world knows of your utter core

so that they may take some inspiration
and find their family, ready to offer salvation

i'm not twenty-two anymore
and yet the memories from that day are embedded in my core

so i pray for but one thing
that my childhood was not lost in vain and instead can bring

light to the problems surrounding childhood misuse
and help children become aware of their potential, despite abuse

---

[5]Kirwan is my paternal family's surname.

39

ABUSE OR MISUSE

my hands are shaking, i feel like i'm being abused again
only i'm not, just used again

by a man who, like the step-father i had
thinks it's ok to use his eyes to grab

hold of a nice view
it's ok if i'm not actually touching you

he says through the malice in his grin
acting like what he's doing isn't a sin

but in a way he was touching me
my innocence, stealing it, pretending like it's free

and it burnt like a 'witch' at the stake into mistrust
again, i'm learning what happens when a man prioritises lust

while you think it's ok to stare me up and down
you neglect to realise how wrong it is, that's why i'm starting to frown

because whilst you might think it's ok
to undress me with your eyes, like i won't say

in that moment where you're stealing a look
you're also creating the path less took

40

the one where i decide
that actually it's not ok to take me for a ride

saying, "you can't stand there and stare
at every corner of my body like it's bare"

where you're taught that what you're doing is wrong
even though you think we're too dumb to use our voices to be strong

you didn't realise that the woman you tried with this time
is unfortunately well versed with this type of crime

you see this has happened to me all before
the same acts as yours just a whole lot more

a step-father who swore to be a man
but instead would wake me up every morning and pan

up and down with his eyes
but also took it further, like i was his prize

a child at the time, i didn't know how to stand up for myself
i spent years laying there letting him abuse me or else

i thought i would be hurting everyone if i stopped concealing
because i was never taught to value what i was feeling

but now i'm not a child
and this time i'm going to use my voice to run wild

on behalf of all children everywhere
who have ever fallen victim to such despair

so you can't sit there and stare at me 'sir'
because i'll make sure i create the biggest stir

to defend my rights
that have finally come to light

thanks to the work of women
who made it their mission

to correct society's misgivings
about our freedom and types of livings

this time i'm not going to let you intimidate me
instead remind you that i can incriminate thee

because just like you want to enjoy your life
i need to be alone without feeling rife

full of fear because of who
a man who thinks it's ok to come on through

and do as he pleases, without any respect
well, i'm here to tell you that i do detect

a form of abuse
although some might term it just a misuse

42

but when a supposed 'man' starts to build habits such as these
they're the stepping stones of grooming, to gain what will eventually please

his sickening acts of molestation
that god forbid will turn into something more brazen

so don't tell me not to worry that he's "not actually touching you"
for years that step-dad was just looking, before he used his hands too

a man that tries to seductively stare you up and down
in an obviously and uninvitingly sexual manner, is a clown

a 'man' who is not worthy of the title
because i will not let people like him ruin the name for those who are vital

to the reputation of our men
because unlike him there are countless good men

who know how to treat us like humans
and not a piece of meat, ready to ruin

whatever some so carelessly squander
reckless and vulgar without even a wonder

as to how your actions impact others you disrespect
but i don't think that even crosses your mind, nor do i expect

these words to change your behaviour
just don't think for a second that you're not putting yourself in danger

43

i told you this would be the path less taken
someone getting away with it before doesn't mean i'll be twice mistaken

abuse doesn't get any double jeopardy
this time you've triggered a memory

reminding me of what happened the last time i remained silent
when that step-dad took my silence as a yes so i had to remain compliant

but i've learnt since then
that was a falsehood created when

i was taught how to put everyone else's needs above my own
and to never make a sound about anything, let alone

anything interfering with the comfort of my mum and her boyfriend
because after mentioning myself at all, i would never hear the end

so i'll say this one last time
before i continue with my rhyme

go back out the door you came
because this time i won't be the same

i'll shout it at the top of my lungs if i have to
call a spade a spade, you're an abuser and i'm bound to

learn that just because you think it didn't cross a line
is not my responsibility to ensure you toe the line

44

you see you're part of a collective that have lesser standards
when it comes to human beings and their slanders

against any woman who cries "me too"
as if we're part of some secret coup

trying to undermine your integrity, when in fact
we're just trying to right wrongs and keep intact

the potential for future generations to grow up safe
to make a difference and change the way that we brave

the enforcement of no means no
and that if you don't like it then you can go

because abuse is abuse
it doesn't matter if it was acute or obtuse

it's not misuse
it's not simply a wrong pen that you did use

it was a moment where you thought of no one but your evil self
and a moment i'll never forget, like a broken trophy on a shelf

there as a reminder of a particular event
only not of something to be proud of, just of something to prevent

from ever happening to me again
which is why i'll passionately complain

B.K

that calling something like this just a misuse
is how so many before have gotten away with abuse

46

grieving the loss of who i could have been
grieving the loss of someone i've never seen

realising i was robbed of the best version of myself
realising who i am now is the result of rescuing myself

sincerely,
the protagonist

47

THERAPY

i stopped going to therapy
because they no longer had the recipe

you see i'm trying to heal from a childhood
that left me without any mild good

well, that's not entirely correct
it blessed me with a means to reflect

on a position where now by contrast
i'm able to appreciate what my life has gotten past

and it's obvious i wouldn't know how good i have it
if it weren't for the times where the pain was rampant

now don't get me wrong, i'm not saying i should be thankful, just grateful
the difference is one belongs to me and the other would be painful

see i realised this on my own
perhaps that's because now i've grown

or because the time for therapy
is now no longer my necessity

although, i have spent years there
so there was a time and place for it, to be fair

48

and so to my therapist i want to say thanks
because without i would not know my own planks

solid and firm
removing the broken ones with worms

by worms i mean bad parents
yes, i know i'm always going on tangents

and i also know you shouldn't bite the hand that feeds you
but if my mum was a farmer then i was the livestock in her rear view

because if one hadn't noticed
she was the worm in my planks that went unnoticed

i'll say it again - ms therapist, thank you for listening in back then
i didn't realise i needed you but i think this is how it should begin, when

you were the first person to offer validation to my feelings
something up until then i did not know would be so healing

but i want to take to life on my own now, give mother nature a go
i feel like it's her turn, she'll have something to say i know

perhaps it can fill a void for the mother i never had
ironic i know but sometimes that's how life works, it's mad

but i guess it's not up to us to control where the dial goes
that illusion belongs to time and i do not wish to be froze

so instead, i'll push forward now that our sessions are at an end
and please know you were more than i knew i needed, almost like a friend

but now that it's at an end, i'd like to try and prove to myself
that therapy and faith is how we gain a better sense of one's self

your trauma doesn't define you

and your pain should never hide you

from the world that we call reality

because in truth we have all suffered as a consequence of our mortality

sincerely,

life

PRETEND

they say it's therapeutic to heal your inner child
so let's take a stroll down memory lane for a while

pretend you're walking into your childhood room
sit down on the bed beside you and reflect on all the doom

younger you is fast asleep
unaware of future you, thoughts now deep

look around the room, memories of a time gone by
and reflect on all the things you thought here, every time you'd cry

feeling totally and always alone
between these four walls you have grown

not in a home you deserved
but in the one that forced you to preserve

as much of you as possible
for the day you do the impossible

now look back at younger you
and say all the things you wish you knew

say, "one day everything will be ok
it might not be right now but you'll find your way"

52

one day you'll run free
creating your own sanctuary

one day you'll be able to smile
without having to worry for a while

one day you'll get out of this place
and you'll use your story to try and grace

time with lessons learnt
to tell the story of how you earnt

freedom, not just physically
but also through healing mentally

one day you'll be happy
walking around westminster abbey[6]

standing in poet's corner[7]
not realising who's now in your corner

not realising how much work you've put in
to eventually become like your own twin

like the version of you, you always wanted
inside those walls that felt utterly haunted

one day you won't be scared
you won't go to bed feeling impaired

---

[6]A church in London, England.
[7]A section inside Westminster Abbey where many celebrated authors,
of varying works, are memorialised and honoured.

53

suffocating from a lack of fresh air
polluted with all this selfish despair

you'll learn how to be happy without a mother
and find comfort in the blessings of another

one day you'll wake up and i promise it won't be here
you'll wake up excited for each day, without fear

of all the beatings, yellings and screaming
of all the stealing of your innocence - defeating

remember when they'd say, "you're so mature for your age"
without realising you're just a child and how they're ripping out a page

from your book called life, in the part where you're just a kid
where they rewrite their own version of how you should bid

for mercy every day
as if it's normal to live this way

no, one day little one
you'll walk out that door and run

for the hills on the other side
where you can finally breathe, not hide

the truth from the world
protecting them from the lies they hurled

54

and horrible actions
stealing from you life's best interactions

one day you'll wake up and the nightmares will be done
you'll think about them now and then but you won't be the one

torn between keeping everyone happy, as you wipe your tears in private
because if anyone saw you'd be beaten just for trying to survive it

pretend you've told younger you what you wish you could have known
blow a kiss goodbye and make peace with everything you had to own

stand up, walk out that door
and leave behind everything you once heavily bore

as you close behind the entrance to your past
remember how long you fought to now be free at last

realise how much you were letting the past hold you back
and walk forward, hand on heart, knowing you're on track

to make younger you happy, grateful for the change
to be everything you ever wanted, free from those chains

it's ok to remember the pain sometimes
as long as it's not stealing from you even more times

where you could be so much happier, living your best life
where you could be helping others getting out of strife

55

where you give younger you everything you ever deserved
healing your inner child and being the adult that you've earned

pretend you're whoever it was you needed but never had growing up
and realise you're now your own hero just instead as a grown up

sometimes your adulthood

must heal your childhood

sincerely,

trauma

PART TWO

PEOPLE
&
PLACES

the who and the where;
of the memories we create
which together can make something great

to travel is to free the mind
of one's perceived unofficial crimes

to which hindered them from seeing
how life could be so freeing

sincerely,
perspective

AUSTRALIAN MADE FROM IMPORTED INGREDIENTS

australian made from imported ingredients
born and raised in sydney whilst to my culture obedient

first, out of force
like all strict parents of course

but second, out of respect
because without even knowing it taught me what to expect

from music when i hear that tuble[8] beat
and suddenly my hips just know how to move with my feet

from food, when i taste chicken
knowing what lemon and garlic will thicken

my appetite and taste for life
because we have age old stories that get us through any strife

from family, when we all gather around a fire
kettle on, serving tea, telling stories of what to aspire

from life, sharing with me the beauty of the emerald isle
because those hills tell more stories than any call could ever dial

but i too love this country
it's a home away from home to put it bluntly

---

[8]A Middle Eastern drum.

immersed in the energy of a culture that is infinite
whilst salvaging my own for future generations – persistent

that's the thing about culture everywhere
it doesn't matter where it's from, there's beauty in its air

i love this country that gave us so much
and also, i love my ancestors who created so much

traditions, customs which make us feel connected
bringing life to those past, present and future – respected

there's nothing like a community where you feel like you belong
dancing and making music to age old folk songs

you see my heart is split in three
first, for my paternal blood, for the country that is my tree

the foundation of my roots
what helps me breathe air into my lungs and hoot

the zaghrouta[9] from the top of these lungs
belly dancing my way through the nights that are young

mixing spices for recipes that trace back to our ancestors
and so second, for my maternal blood, for my very own predecessors

which brings me to split three
for the country that housed me

---

[9]An ululation sound, typical of Middle Eastern culture,
used as a means to express celebration.

offering up a sun that warmed my soul
guided my mornings and helped my family enrol

in that better way of life
like so many before, running away to this wild life

i don't know what my families would have done otherwise
i'll try to never take for granted this blessing in disguise

so here's to the country that raised me
whilst affording me the chance to maintain the cultures that made me

it always was and always will be
and altogether i am so grateful, truly

they started wars in our homelands, our ancestors' backyards

and used it as a playground for their unmarked facades

sincerely,

teta w jiddo[10]

---
[10]Arabic words meaning grandmother and grandfather.

B.K

FALASTEEN

falasteen[11]
for so many you now go unseen

but there was a time
when your existence wasn't a crime

yet now you have two roles to play
to both exist and to stay

if not for our ancestors, then at least for this generation
because we're trying so hard to retain our connection

to a land that was loved and lost
at, might i add, such an immeasurable cost

so much people in pain
yet apparently that was all for some premeditated gain

but that's not what this poem is about
i'm not here to talk politics, to try and sort it out

those whirlwinds of emotions that come from both sides
no, i want to talk about something much deeper than those tides

see they come and go like the waves on the shore
but our belief in our culture is something that never recedes at all

---

[11]The Arabic word for Palestine.

65

B.K

from our music to our dance
our thobes[12] and belief in chance

we hold onto our faith
and pass down what lessons we acquired in fate

now we might be on the other side of the world
but that doesn't mean we won't hold onto this pearl

of information passed down to us
from teta w jiddo to which they entrust

the continuation of our line
that no wall can ever confine

because it's free falasteen
no matter how much they call it a dream

and i don't expect them to understand
this undying desire to feel a connection to the land

but i can feel it in my bones
with the beat of the tuble and its tones

its sound ignites this primal instinct
that proves we will never go extinct

because without even being taught
about a culture that is now heavily distraught

---

[12]Traditional Palestinian dress.

66

we feel it in our knees
it lives rent free in our olive trees

like the dabke[13] when we fall into line
even if it's your very first time

you just know what to do
how to feel, it's so true

and although they try to deny it
that we were living there in quiet

until external selfish needs
became the plea of everyone despite their creed

so don't try and pin us against each other
jewish, christian, muslim, we are sisters and brothers

and i see what they're doing, creating anarchy within
because they know a house that's divided falls from its own sin

but i keep telling them our connection to land is deeper than that
that's why almost a hundred years on and we're still looking at

how we can move forward
but not in the way that we're ordered

rather in a means of recovery
in what remains of our ancestry

---

[13]A Levantine Arab folk dance.

and we're never going to give up, i hope they can hear that in our voices
a land flowing with milk and honey as the remedy to our causes

and we will come home one day
after they're finished with this game they play

because whilst they're busy playing chess with all our lives
it doesn't matter where we've sought refuge, we're keeping our
culture alive

to the innocent children in all of this,

may you one day be able to play together
may you one day live in peace forever

and to the ones that have lost their lives since october seven
may you be spending your days happy up in heaven

sincerely,
humanity

i leave you with a dream where we can all finally say
jewish, christian, muslim – we stand together come what may

if not for humanity, then at the very least for the children
the ones being buried in the same ground they're fighting over,
leaving in ruins

sincerely,
gaza

70

IRELAND

ireland the emerald isle
you've had a special place in my heart for a while

giving me a culture
that saved me from a vulture

not through conventional means
but rather through your comedic genes

which seems to run so rampant
through your beautiful smiles that never dampen

despite how much it rains
it never seems too much a pain

no matter what life throws your way
you're always a hardy bunch ready to say

"god never closed one door without opening another"[14]
and even if you don't believe that, you get on without a bother

because that's what the british army taught you
no matter how many times you're kicked down, they cannot stop you

you're an imperial bunch
a play on words i know but i have a hunch

---

[14]A saying my grandfather often uses.

71

that your collective good form and high spirits
is what keeps you all going, despite the imposed limits

chasing cattle down roads that are covered in cracks
spreading every message of hope imbedded with craic[15]

and before anyone says it, i don't mean that kind
you cheeky fecker, read between the rhyme

i'm joking of course
something an irish family teaches without force

how to not take life so seriously
because that's how you end up so wearily

hating each morning
despite what it's adorning

no, your type could never do that
you all see so much magic even in a stray cat

superstitious, some of you, yes
but it's more of just a mess

because that too is a part of your good humour
to be honest, ireland is my total cure

it's the greatest gift, just what i needed
a culture that never fails to make me smile when impeded

B.K

---

[15]Irish slang for a "good time" and can be synonymous
with the terms "news" and "fun".

from all of life's ups and downs
the craic is always there picking up my crown

singing happiness back into my giggle
plucking away those weeds with your fiddle

a rich and beautiful history
full of bittersweet victory

ireland is full of so much beauty
its folk imbedded with utter duty

to the betterment of their country
that no army can ever take from thee

you're always down for a pint
when one's reality just isn't sitting right

which helps provide that extra warmth
when one's laughter isn't quite so forth

taking over the night
assisting in their plight

but that's not your only means
of helping each other dream

you're a culture of people who care
and will do your best for anyone, despite where

73

B.K

and perhaps it's no myth at all
that our irish culture can never fall

because despite those who made our language illegal
and seeming to think of our people as feeble

we've always remained strong
pushing forward through every wrong

and that's what makes us so unique
a culture that survived so much defeat

and still in the emerald isle
you all carry on with a smile

getting on with each day like it's the bees' knees and spiders' ankles[16]
in ireland it doesn't matter how bad life gets, they're never tangled

because that's always what the irish do
living life the best they can with a good cup of brew

---

[16]An idiom commonly used in Ireland to express something as being (or thought of as being) excellent.

B.K

rolling emerald meadows

reminds me of the emerald isle's fellows

of the people who make that country so great

that find beauty in anything, despite distaste

because it doesn't matter how bad life gets

we're always willing to do our best

sincerely,

an irish perspective

POET'S CORNER

i stood in poet's corner
not yet understanding the honour that was in order

all these brilliant minds
having so much to say in their beautiful rhymes

what a shame their ideas had to come to an end
i guess one day everyone runs out of ink in their pen

which inspires me now
to write it all down

everything that i hear
before death impales me with its spear

but i take solace in knowing
that poetry lives on without loaning

time from anyone, not even ourselves
because that's the beauty in poetry, it lives on, on our shelves

it's magic on paper
magic that lives on throughout the ages, like a favour

that we return to life for the beauty that was heard
that not everyone hears, so instead poets yearn

76

for everyone to listen
to what's being written

with pen and paper
hoping you'll discover it sooner rather than later

you see places like poet's corner exist
because humanity needs poetry to persist

through this world's unfathomable crimes
that enslaves us in a mindset of thinking that reality just confines

when in truth, whilst often times that may be the case
most of us just don't know how to slow down our pace

enough to listen to everything in between
the meaning between the lines, creating your dream

see there's magic in almost everything
and i believe that's the song poets are trying to sing

HISTORY

"these walls have ears"[17]
and so these walls could tell stories for years

that's why i hear magic in their cracks
their crevices are full with so much that racks

my brain through a timeline of history
making me ponder as to what these walls have seen, like a mystery

it's not just a church or a castle
it's a textbook of the past, sharing with me what once did dazzle

these halls of time
which fill my soul with so much rhyme

because there's beauty to be heard
in the energy that fills these walls, like a bird

and i wish i could see it
push my hand against the wall and fall between it

as if travelling back in time
dancing at a ball, laughing and sipping wine

they say curiosity killed the cat
so like pullman[18] alluded, i better get back

B.K

78

---

[17]A commonly used expression.
[18]Phillip Pullman, an English writer.

to my own time, my own point in history

where questions go unanswered and i stay in love with said mystery

death is not what i fear

it's the loss of my loved ones, the day they're not near

sincerely,

youth

GRANDAD

grandad our saint
intrinsically imprinted like a canvas' paint

a blessing disguised as an angel with life
a debt we could never repay, no matter how rife

his life is like no other
a man without a bother

never a complaint
and never running late

the hero in everyone's story
saving the day with all his inventory

grandad to the rescue
there's no better man to bless you

with his presence, his energy
he could light up a room with such synergy

making a dull day
simply fade away

as if the light was always there
but he was just the first one to care

B.K

the world will be sorry when it has to let you go
because it knows it will never again see another like so

a heart of gold, a mind so bright
there is always so much of his wonderous insight

there's not a day that goes by where i don't fear your loss
because without your love my heart will become like moss

you see every family needs someone like grandad
the one who puts meaning to the "grand" in grandad

i just wonder how heaven is doing without you
a great loss the day you were sent for our view

but like you, they did us a favour or two
saving us all from a life with a dark hue

the foundation of this family would be nothing without you
together with granny, you are both our glue

i hope that one day more of your sayings will prove right
they always serve for such motivational insight

he'd say, "it's not about the castles you build that fall
it's about the ones that eventually and inevitably stand tall"

never quit, he does always encourage
life takes great patience and he's right, maintain courage

82

because eventually one castle will have to stand
it's all just trial and error until one honours the command

what a love our hearts have known
to call this grandad our own

with your beautiful wife
you gave us all such a loving life

i'll never know a love more pure
like that of yours, you two are such a lure

inspirational on all accounts
if only life didn't have to run out

i dread the day
that you'll have to go away

and i hope you know just how much we all love you
everyone knows you gave us heaven on earth, i'd argue

thank yous aren't enough for our grandad
so i'm giving you this poem, before one day i'm too sad

but like ed said, "a heart that's broke is a heart that's been loved"[19]
so thank you grandad for everything, our dove

---

[19]Lyrics from the song *Supermarket Flowers* by Ed Sheeran,
an English singer-songwriter.

GRANNY

there's no greater woman i've ever known
and when it comes to fashion, there's style in everything she owns

class personified in this woman of duty
there's never a day where we aren't in awe of her beauty

her smile is like a garden
solitary beauty like that of the arden[20]

she's embedded in my being
as if without there is no seeing

because she is inherently the source of our own life
bringing us all on a journey, details of the highlife

she teaches us how to make the most
out of everything that we shall host

live not in temptation
instead deliver through concentration

like granny said, "who better to see me looking fine
than my dearest family and loving husband of mine"

she taught me to take pride in every image
that i present to the world, in splendour and envisage

---

[20]A great forest.

84

she said, "self-respect, it starts in the home
and when fostered can stay with you, through to when you're grown"

that's how granny presents
dressed to the nines, always intense

you live only once
and she makes sure she looks like a stunt

half her age it seems
because she looks a dream

eighty-five according to her certificate
but when she smiles she looks infinite

as if she always will go on
because she's found the secret to look upon

where we learn that life's best ingredient is happiness
and if we're lucky enough to find it, take it and marry it

that's what granny did, not hungry for money or anything material
but she is a lover of fashion, jewellery and shoes, let's be real

a style queen in her own right
no one compares to her presence and excite

for the life she leads and the family she loves
she is our saint and our very own dove

if the idea of your death scares me this much

then i utterly fear the day reality becomes such

sincerely,

love

86

i will keep you alive in my routine
in my footsteps, with my tea

everyday i will live as you did live
rising early in the morning, ready to give

sincerely,
honour

DEAR DAD

dear dad, i wish i understood you more
i mean before i grew up and tried to decipher your core

you were so young when i came along
learning on the job, experience would prolong

a journey for you
with a daughter, plus a few

where you tried to figure out the best path to run down
because you didn't realise the road walked was better all round

you spent years trying to learn how
one thing time never changed though is that your heart is worth a bow

growing up there wasn't a thing you wouldn't do
for anyone and everyone around to whom you knew

and not much has changed
other than how now you try to exchange

some of your own kindness freely given
for yourself now that you're out of prison

you see i took a while to understand that everyone has their journey
and so i didn't realise that my own father required some mercy

after i ran away, i was so angry asking why
you'd ever pick someone that always made me cry

but you were just twenty-one
youth cut short, suddenly removing all fun

because now you had a baby in your sights
and life wasn't going to just tell you how to get it right

and i'm sorry for all my pain
that turned into your further gain

i guess i was trying to heal
and i'm still learning how to open and close that seal

you were challenged with a life that at times was hard
one too many unlucky hands dealing each card

cards life dealt
that didn't care how you felt

and you were dealt a dirty hand
which naturally had you feeling scammed

but i'm proud of you for trying, you've never given up
although i'm sure you've thought about it after all the hiccups

dear dad, i love you
i've always held you in virtue

and i want you to know that you were right
mum would have won if it weren't for how tight

our bond was from the beginning, you always gave me hope
so that even when you weren't around i waited to elope

to run away with life and marry its opportunities
because i'd lost enough time drowning in its cruelties

but this time i hope it's different
i want my father by my side - magnificent

because we've got time to make up for and we've only just begun
london was but a start to the father and daughter fun

so please live your life like a parade
show the world what granny and grandad made

an irishman indeed
full of so much seeds

that you can plant in your farm
and finally you'll be in no harm

because you're my dad, pure and good
i've finally come to terms and understood

that not everything is perfect, that's not how it's meant to be
the sooner we both learn that the more we'll be free

B.K

and i want you to know that your existence
is what always fuelled my resistance

in never giving up or giving into sin
because your love and kindness would always help me win

thank you for teaching me the lessons i first needed
i can confidently say that without i wouldn't have pleaded

for a second chance, to run away
to start again and find you all midway

in a race to correct everything that was done wrong
learning from the mistakes and continuing on

and now that we've got our second chance
let's get this show on the road, it's time to do our own dance

dear dad, you're my king
thank you for everything

THE ELDEST DAUGHTER

to be the eldest daughter
can sometimes feel like slaughter

your youth often sacrificed, accelerating into your adulthood
and once grown we try to then recover our childhood

after spending years feeling like we were some other
kind of stand in substitute mother

then they wonder why so many of us don't want kids
because we already raised ones that weren't ours to begin with

but maybe some of us do, the lucky few
those that don't feel like their time is owing - due

to be repaid because their youth was stolen
while they spent their prime years on hands and knees swollen

for all that extra load
carrying around on your own

i know not all parents mean it
in fact, there are those that need it

and perhaps my experience has made me bias
to my interpretation of an eldest daughter's riots

B.K

but this is my little plea
for all parents with an eldest daughter, she

needs you to take care of her
because whilst she's your first learning curve, there isn't a spare of her

to take her place when you're older and grey
waiting for her to take care of you while you sit there and pray

giving thanks for the daughter that looks after you
now that she's returned to take care of you

care, it's part of the job description
the only trouble is we start too early in our position

and the retirement age doesn't compensate
instead, you just have to work and then wait

for your turn, if you can call it that
to reassess the life you're looking at

before it goes past the point of no return
like the phantom[21], that means you never have your turn

and so another eldest daughter loses out
on the luxuries afforded to those without

the pressures of being the first born
where time is taken from your youth and torn

---

[21]A main character in the musical production, *The Phantom of The Opera*.

93

from any prospect of having an average childhood
because apparently our siblings need double the motherhood

and to those where this pressure was endured through love
i hope it all resulted in a stronger bond above

all else, for the sake of family
because then perhaps it was worth all the calamity

but for those that endured such pressures without love
i hope you recovered the loss and learnt to put yourself above

the removal of your freedom, your independence, your spirit
learnt how to rebuild your life with creativity and no limit

you know, it's a shame life isn't more fair
but i guess that's why artists have so much to share

94

CHURCH

my church is planet earth and its ceilings are the sky
it's not just those buildings where i go to pray and cry

but rather all around
in every corner where life can be found

now it's not that church makes me sad
in fact, being there makes my heart rather glad

to be listening to all those beautiful voices
god's music emanates through my soul of choices

which, might i add, influences me so much
particularly in how i express my thoughts that i trust

but no, my church is in nature
in the way the winter wind freezes my hair like a glacier

cold against my face
reality reminding me of its pace

while the summer sun warms my hands
inspiring me to conjure up demands

requesting i lead a life full and achieve
motivate and reach, that's why i strongly believe

regardless of what you call it, god is everywhere
listening, chanting, hoping that we compare

how life feels outdoors
when our bare feet are running along the shores

when leaves ring around our fingers
and the flowers stay and softly linger

subtle reminders of the beauty in their petals
a metaphor for life in that we should never settle

because like the flower that blooms
before eventually dying in gloom

with a little bit of love and care
it will eventually always return to air

showing how we can all shine
with patience and in our own time

and just because that's not always
doesn't mean we won't have more ways

to drink from life's good juice
fill ourselves up with the water of use

i learnt all of this from nature
which is why i say my church is in mother nature

GOD

god might be in the sky
but also in the wings of the birds that use it to fly

think about that for a second
when do you feel closest to god – i beckon

is it when you're walking along the shore
feeling that primal instinct in your core

or is it when you're watching the waves crash
wanting to feel it run through your hands - alas

is it when you wake up in the morning
and for the first time you aren't yawning

or is it the day you actually enjoy your job
because for once it doesn't quite feel like a job

is it the moment when you realise that true family is the
ultimate goal
and when you find it, realise it creates a happiness which fills that
bottomless hole

or the day where for some unknown reason
you listen to a song that makes you cry like the wet season

see the problem with simply institutionalising religion
is that the average person isn't able to even

feel god all around
rather than only on the ground

because although you can find god there in prayer
god is also everywhere

listen to god in that beautiful sound
those birds in the sky make, above the ground

or from the trees in the wind as they sway back and forth
they're making god's music, in the south and in the north

and also in the east and in the west
the sound might use a different tone but no less

god is not limited to the ground and the sky
spread your mind's wings, fall into the energy and try

to resonate with life's frequencies
it's crazy when you listen to the music of god's secrecies

but they're only secret for as long as you let them
if you open your heart and mind, you'll soon hear them beckon

because god is everywhere
call it what you may, i don't care

98

god, the universe
it doesn't matter as long as you don't head to your hearse

before experiencing the true beauty of life
remember perception is subjective so maybe think twice

the next time you pick up a flower
and only see the beauty in what it may currently empower

as if its beautiful face of petals and smell
is any more beautiful than the journey it took to shed its shell

and that's where you'll find god
first in the flower but then in the odd

yet wonderful things that happen
along the way as you'd imagine

because it really is the little things that make the big things seem so great
like a reward after a journey that took you so long to take

when the destination teaches you that beauty is along the way
as well as in the reward of what you earnt, after you pay

like i said, call it what you may
religion, spirituality, whatever you say

i just implore you to open up your heart to the magic of life
it's hidden in the simple things so many of us take for granted, it's rife

jim carrey said it best, "why not take a chance on faith"[22]
even if not for religion, take a chance and wait

slow down and focus on the beauty all around you
and i hope one day you tell me that a higher voice found you

[22]A quote from Jim Carrey, a Canadian-American
actor, during his Commencement Speech at
Maharishi University of Management in 2014.

THE WRONG GUY

i'm with the wrong guy
that's what keeps making me cry

i've just been in denial
for more than a little while

but it's because i've invested so much time
hoping one day you'd always be mine

but i forgot that sometimes adults can get it wrong
that is mentally what has been taking me so long

admitting that sometimes things can be just lessons
not meant to be anything more than a session

of experience, after all that is the best teacher
i guess i was just hoping you wouldn't be my preacher

showing me what not to do again
apparently, life lessons come hidden like chains

we have to learn how to break them
that's why letting go feels like mayhem

because after being together for so long
you can't help but prolong

101

the inevitable cessation
to what you felt could have been a beautiful creation

between two loved souls
but instead, now you have to control

how you handle yourself moving forward
exiting a relationship is very awkward

almost like a baby learning how to walk
your heart has to learn all over again how to talk

to new comers, asking so many questions
like what's your favourite colour before deciding on first impressions

then embarking on a few more years
before the blur of not knowing if they're the one clears

oh, how we hate to get things wrong
i guess that's a part of human nature we could have forgone

because making mistakes is part of life's journey
it's what makes us all full of so much yearning

to find out that the true meaning of life is about lessons
is a hard pill to swallow, the harshness of which we try to lessen

so when a relationship comes to an end
there feels like there's so much that needs to mend

one of you may feel indifferent
and the other may always miss it

but life always has a way of reminding us
about lessons not properly learnt, by reteaching us

and for now, i want to finish by saying
if you feel the same way, stop wasting

time if you're with the wrong guy
stop trying to force the issue and try

conserving your days, months and even years
because you're drowning in so many unforeseen fears

fears that you'll hurt him, that you'll get it all wrong
but when do you stop, take a chance and sing your own song

A LETTER TO AN EX

three o'clock on a sunday afternoon
and i feel like we're on a dock, hiding from the moon

because we know what comes next
a bit of darkness in a crest

but i'm praying that you'll be fine
even if you're the type that doesn't drink wine

now i'm sure you think i'm trying to take away the sun
when in reality i've just realised i'll never be the mother of your son

because unlike these poems that flow from my mind
we're not natural, we don't grow, together we're blind

there's no honey in our taste
nothing sweet to use as paste

on the foundation for our future
which is important in this life if you're my suitor

and i'm sorry it took me so long to create
an understanding in my mind, i'm just a little late

at realising that although yes, we were best friends
it was far too soon for this to be the end

104

of giving up on true love, settling for books
to act as compensation for our lack of hooks

and now this isn't meant to be a bashing
i'm not here to write you some sort of thrashing

but i hope you know i wanted to marry my best friend
to be lost in and amongst a love found in laughter, till the end

yet something went wrong
suddenly 'culture' influenced a mindset that altered us along

a path for destruction
and we deserve better than a love drowning in corruption

i guess what i'm trying to say is thank you
the years are not lost on me, i wasn't trying to prank you

we were both just young and couldn't see
that unless there is fuel for fire, we shouldn't be

and i pray one day you find her
the one that becomes your binder

to all good things in life
and that you make her your wife

because if that had to have been me
there's only one-way things would have turned out to be

B.K

a myriad of lies
and some countless tries

of me forcing the issue
for a love just because we wish to

and then mix that with religion
one muslim, one christian

i'm not saying that was the reason it couldn't work, it could
but when you mix that altogether, i just knew it never would

like the venom in a snake once it has decided to bite
it was just time to say goodbye because we lost our light

but i will always wish you well in this life, this journey
i pray after everything you've been through you live a life so worthy

of all the blessings that make one reflect
with a smile on a life full of happy memories that you got to collect

106

HOME

growing up, i always hated leaving people's homes that we were visiting
because the 'home' we were going back to was nothing worth envisioning

going to see people was like a free pass to therapy
because it afforded me an opportunity of peace, momentarily

so when i tell you there is a special kind of peace to be found
when you grow up, move out and are free to roam around

but are happy when the time comes for you to leave
because for once the place you're returning to is free of pain - believe

peace, it definitely is worthy of being called
because my mental health has finally made a truce that has enthralled

me in the simple things
i appreciate my life now for all that it brings

and perhaps i wouldn't know this luxury
if not for the pain that was once forced upon me

that's not to say that everything that happened was ok
but rather to appreciate the silver lining, come what may

when i tell you home is not just where the heart is
that's because it's also the place where you don't feel starved in

where you feel at peace, where it's your preferred place to be
and i pray all those who never had a home, find it and see
life is so beautiful when you have that place where you feel free

oh, but you are beautiful, don't you see

your pain, although sad, has been memorialised for an eternity

because where you could no longer see truly

a poet saw you as a poem and immortalised your beauty

sincerely,

poetry

PART THREE

LIFE

the condition of existence;
filled with a myriad of lessons along journeys taken
that is, of course, until you reach your final destination

according to probability you have years left

but according to chance you have wasted them like theft

sincerely,

time

THE SECOND GENERATION

too second generation to feel like a local
yet too local to feel like a second generation

as if dichotomy personified
inside my mind of pride

i speak the language of a culture i don't feel connected to
yet don't speak the language of a culture i feel connected to

you see i love my parentage
and even the subsequent advantage

that comes of my families' actions
as they sought so many retractions

of a culture to which they love
but had to salvage and put us above

abroad in a foreign land
seeking refuge at the hand

of a place they would soon call home
but first take years to settle in and roam

finding a balance between learning the nuances
of an entirely new culture yet feeling like the chances

afforded to them in their new home
giving them a choice between retaining or being shown

meant they would always feel different
out of place or indifferent

thank you to my families' persistence
in seeking a better life, despite the inconsistence

between their comfort levels
and all their new revels

because at the same time
of wanting to remain true to your own culture's chime

both they and i
have had to make a choice and try

to decide where we fit in
is it here or within

a mindset that helps us reminisce
of a place where we all so dearly miss

and yet what they miss doesn't even exist anymore
you see if you leave a place long enough it changes at its core

now i spend my days eating the food of my ancestors
whilst wearing the clothes of another culture, our benefactors

and i'm not saying i shouldn't be grateful
i know that without i would be so hateful

of the life our families would have been forced to lead
because of the wars they would continue to face, being forced to plead

for a better way of life
which in truth is the sacrifice they made twice

first, giving up their homeland
second, giving up their own plan

of the life they once dreamed
before everything was stolen beneath their seams

but instead, gave that all of up to watch us grow
a life full of seeds to which we can now sow

seeds they harvested with their own hands
gifting them to us to use for our own plans

to head into a new direction
building, creating a life without rejection

calling us the second generation
the ones who feel lost and yet found in this new cultural demonstration

where we learn to appreciate both sides
those that came before us and those who gave us a means to decide

i am from the seeds of the olive trees whose roots grow
intertwined with the shamrocks that decorate the foundations i sow

sincerely,
the celtic arab

116

MIXED RACE

mixed race - two cultures, one body
to feel drawn in two directions and yet also like you're a nobody

too much like my father's side to be like my mother
and yet too much like my mother's side to be like my father

they say your skin doesn't look like you're from either or
your hair could be a resemblance of both, it's too similar to say for sure

and no, before anyone says it, we're not confused
but i can't explain how we feel proud and yet bemused

feeling grateful to be afforded a safe place to call home
and yet crying because i want a place to call my own

back where my grandparents grew up
where the trees saw my ancestors wake up

each and every morning adding stepping stones to cultures
that built proud histories full of so much colours

from generation upon generation of hard-working people
who built places known for its art that could equal

a louvre[23] of their own
of which all the contents they would own

---

[23]An art museum in Paris, France.

117

from our food, clothes, music, idioms
altogether making a rich history infinitum

i can't explain to you why learning the language makes me cry
or why i'm so desperately writing down all these recipes in time

before what i fear the most happens
i lose my only validation of what i fathom

to be this deep potential for an unwritten connection
in my dna, like some sort of self-woven obsession

with who i could have been
if i didn't feel like there were two of me

one day i feel more like my paternal side
and then the next dominated internally by my maternal side

picture this
growing up where your parents raised you in bits

one arguing that to be strict was the only way
whilst the other assured that, that would have the opposite display

of what they were looking for in a daughter alone
one shouting that she can never go out without a chaperone

whilst the other cried freedom as a means for independence
and in response said you'll lose her in your dependence

118

B.K

on archaic ways, believing them to be more harmful than good
but they never saw eye to eye, however i withstood

i learnt to find a means of balance
to love the best parts of both in one palace

where i adorn my life with the best parts of both worlds
and marry them together, creating the best part of my own world

where i learn how to make all the food
dance to the music in our clothes, offering a mood

that settles me in peace
where i become like my grandparents, using the same idioms as if a lease

from both sides of my heritage, where we pass it down, one to the next
and one day we'll realise being mixed doesn't deprive that
it just makes us complex

119

THE RAT RACE

i'm finally winning the race of running away from home
only to find out there is another race that never should've been condoned

a clogged up coronary
feeling like high way robbery

of both the mind and of the heart
because society is tearing them apart

from each other where they belong
but instead, are being dragged up along

a rat race mindset
that's drowning our highest

order of family values
that wants us to add to what devalues

anything that takes us away from the rat race
that way we're only focused on the illusion of a pace

that apparently advances our life's potential
whilst ignoring that we're not here forever, it's intentional

it's corporation's needs above everyone else's
because they forget how to be at all selfless

they forget our worth as human beings is all made equal
and instead of sharing, they're trying to create a sequel

a second life, a part two
like the ancient egyptians but haven't they taught you

there is nothing you can take
no material goods you can rake

up into your bank account
piling in any amount

is futile if you're not gathering the only thing we can take with us
memories of a lifetime full and within us

of a time and of a place
where we laughed at our own pace

we should be focused on what brings a smile to everyone around
sometimes selflessness teaches us how to sound

in this life, mr rat race, that you're trying to control
but i'm just wondering how you think you'll be let out on parole

for all your wrongdoings, treating people like this
we have families too, we're people in crisis

at the brink of eternal disfunction
unless we stop now and learn how to function

B.K

as one with everyone
benefiting all, not just one

so what's it going to be mr rat race
shall we begin again or remain in these straits of chase

nothing in this world makes sense

when its primary concern is to be run by cents

sincerely,

greed

NOT A ROMANTIC

i'm not a romantic
i want to be but my heart is too frantic

instead of beating for love
it spent too long being beaten to 'love'

those who should have loved me unconditionally
a mother and a step-father who raised me conditionally

used to their own advantage
bruised, cut up until i needed a bandage

to heal all the inflicted wounds
on a heart that just wanted to swoon

over a life filled with love
which could have dressed me with a romantic glove

put on for life's best display
to witness what some wonderful people have to portray

but i have no room in my heart to enjoy or entertain
anyone i meet, like a boy who could pertain

for a story that we could write together
and hopefully create a little piece of forever

124

because my heart was already filled with so much betrayal
and so i fear that i might always be rather frail

when it comes to being a romantic because i built my wall up high
and i'm not sure i'll ever meet someone who'll climb it and then try

to remove it brick by brick
each one representing a kick

that i took along the way
learning a lesson and then storing that memory away

as a reminder to protect myself
against all non-self

against whatever might try to poke holes in my wall
because unless you're willing to get down on my level and crawl

i'm not sure we'll get to the finish line
because if you're trying to run, i'll never keep up in time

because i'm too scared to give second chances
i did that once with those who raised me but all that gave was enhances

on all the emotions that i had already felt
i should have known a love once lost was already dealt

with the judgement of guilty
but i'm always one who will be

feeling bad for making someone question their behaviour
as if it's not bad enough having to be my own saviour

see i never hold anyone accountable
because how dare i make my feelings pronounceable

but i'm finally learning how to not sit in discomfort
because i'm too worried about removing someone else's comfort

but unfortunately, that has cost me oh so much
like a romantic heart that i wish i could just touch

to remind her that it's ok to try again
especially this time because i think i might have found a man

who wants to climb my wall and he's almost there
ready to crawl with me despite my despair

if time could be bought

how often would it be sought

sincerely,

the angel of death

WHEN DEATH COMES KNOCKING

i've seen death knock on one's door
i've seen an almost lifeless body strewn across the floor

i've seen what happens when death comes knocking
the reality of the pain in that you never know who's clocking

a mother falling, overwhelmed with fear
a father devastated, defeated but yet near

a sister who is strong but broken hearted
because she almost watched her brother leave this world, as if departed

i've seen death knock on one's door
and how the human life tries to implore

to convince it that they're far too early
to go home and come back later when they're not so burly

allowing one a second chance
a new perspective on how to enhance

the quality of life now that you appreciate its finality
now that it taught you the hard truth about reality

i've seen death knock on one's door
and sometimes it doesn't always walk back out that door

128

B.K

it doesn't always leave empty handed
more often than not it takes what was taken for granted

leaving others behind holding on to mere memories
of those gone, buried in cemeteries

but for the lucky few who escape death's wrath
i hope you use your second chance for the better path

the acceptance of our mortality

is a harder pill to swallow than any reality

sincerely,

impermanence

130

THIRTY

why the rave about being in your twenties
i wish i knew back then how to make my thoughts worth the pennies

you see it's true what they say about what happens when you turn thirty
suddenly you care less, love more and then the world is at your mercy

knowledge in abundance, confidence so high
everything in your life just slowly starts to comply

with your hopes and dreams that you've been working on so keen
building up your castle, getting ready for it to gleam

and now it's finally time to really fight
show the world the route of your chosen flight

you see your twenties were your playground
a place to sit and find your own sound

until you can truly listen
in your thirties, that's when you start to glisten

from all the lessons learnt, heart breaks and love lost
now you start to shine in your new lease on life, decked out in cost

it took you time to get here and effort to rise
but aren't you so proud of all your cries

you didn't bottle up and let it sink in
you drowned it out and learnt how to swim

so now you can see how we should breathe
learning how to walk the tightrope and not seethe

if only we knew back then how to be patient and true
at a time when all we wanted was to party and push through

life is what you make it, a saying so veracious
so open up your mind and let it run flirtatious

because this is when you fall in love with your life
something you thought you'd never do yet now you're your own wife

committed to your own pillar of strength in your independent stance
once you realised that life is just lessons learnt and a tyranny of chance

so tell me again how our twenties should win
when life seems to get better after your thirties begin

and i've heard it just keeps getting better with age
a word we're taught to hate but you see it's full of such rage

not in a bad way, no it's great
age is full of so much joy you can create

i just wish i knew this sooner; they say hindsight is always key
but perhaps the contrast in perspective is what set me free

so how do i tell you, those waiting in fear
that it's not the end of the world now that thirty is near

your twenties won't be forgot
but your thirties are where you can now do everything you once could not

life has its mysterious ways
of filling our life with turmoil and yet haze

and once we see through it, our eyes open wide
ready to finally see, as if for the first time with pride

rather than seeing the world through their eyes
you're finally free to build your own life - make it your prize

so i'll stop wishing now to go back and restart
because the truth is how could we have known if we never even cart

each and every one of us has a trailer to pull
a load brimmed with lessons - learn them and be full

these are our tools to carnation
once learnt they are the keys to remove starvation

you no longer have to go hungry searching for meaning
now that you've learnt in your thirties you can eat without grieving

tick each life lesson off as a right not a cross
because even if you get it wrong, it is not a loss

133

B.K

life is all about making mistakes
and patience is what it really takes

but hey, your thirties rang, they said to tell you it's ok
they said life gets better, this is where the real party presses play

MODEST FASHION

why modest fashion
well, my body i want to ration

away from prying eyes
away from anyone imagining some sort of prize

and to keep it for my heart
because i want to be the primary witness to my art

you see growing up my body was used
taken advantage of ensued

and so i swore one day
when that all went away

that i'd claim back my body, my gift
something that for so long felt at risk

so that no one can stare
unless i deem it to be fair

now my body is only used
in whatever way i choose

which brings me to my next point
your body, your choice, regardless if you disappoint

whether it is or is not modestly
dress the way you like, personally

so if you're happy with the way that you look
then as we say in arabic, mabrouk[24]

because at the end of the day
happiness should be your main point of play

your sense of fashion should be an engagement
with your sense of self, your identity - a statement

style is an expression of one's freedom of mind
your free spirit that's intertwined

which is why i love those who dress as they please
which is why i choose modesty because it puts me at ease

i now find so much joy in what i wear
and remember, those of us that choose this are not covering up in despair

it's a choice, as it should remain
and to those who wish to use their bodies to retain

a certain level of mystery
subjectively applied, influenced by their history

remember, there is liberty in enclosure
just as there too is liberty in exposure

---

[24]An Arabic expression used to express one's congratulations.

the freedom of choice is the true beauty here
allow everyone to dress as they wish without fear

so to answer your question, why modest fashion
because i dress in whatever way fuels me with passion

to lead a life that charges my batteries
and gives me happiness not measured by flatteries

disregarding all those who say
"you look like a grandma", dressed that way

and i found such a life in modest fashion
now that's not to say you will but for me i certainly can't fathom

feeling the peace that i finally do
in dressing the way that i used to

back when i tried to follow every trend through
pleasing everyone but myself; many of us i'm sure feel this too

see modesty also taught me a sense of compassion
for one's natural beauty which society often deems to lack attraction

which is just not true
the way god made you is beautiful too

all of this is why modesty has become my aesthetical standard
because it taught me how to embrace being utterly candid

LUCK

luck - it isn't what most people think it is
and many of you have heard it said countless times before this

but luck is not the boundless fortune of suddenness fate
rather the composition of hard work for preparation's sake

so that when opportunity indeed does knock
you are ready to present in haste, round the clock

to the next generation of troubled teens
allow me to remind you of one simple deed

yours is a tale both untold and yet tried
dichotomy i know but remember your time has not dried

you may hate your current circumstances to which you cannot dictate
rest assured you aren't the first defeatist of your kind to sit there and wait

to see what your life will hold
but you're forgetting that, that is up to what you can mould

see time is of the essence, an enemy to which you must tame
upon whence your mind becomes intertwined with your intricate frame

your eyes will see life in this ever-serving light
as a cruel peace that comes like the calm before each night

i've learnt that you can and will make it past any undulated task
fulfilled as you hold your head like a boundless and forceful mast

just as a fern may rise with pride
so too may your endeavours with your persistent stride

some may call this good luck
as opposed comparatively to just luck

but just luck, like most things in our lives
is subjectively all up to your own good graces and pride

will you show up and compete, work away at the grime
or will you show not the world but yourself that you are time

meaning time is not what is done to you but rather what you do with time
despite what it tries to make of you, the result is your own chime

yes, that is what darwish[25] has asked and like the topic of this question
time has advised you a task pressing with intention

like its counterpart, luck is what you make of it
so take both it and time and see what you can create with it

will you sit there and let it pass you
or will you mould it and let it enhance you

like the time you do not seize or will you stand up and take it
life has and always will be what you make it

---

[25]Mahmoud Darwish, a Palestinian Poet.

you see luck is the calm before the storm
where you must choose between chaos or good form

meaning, your story is written by your own pen
however, filled with the ink of a thousand good men

yes, my good friend
it is up to you how your story must end

it is up to you what you write
so if you please, grace your pages with stories of might

try, try as you may
and remember luck always comes down to your power of play

EMPATHY

"no one will ever know the violence it took, to become this gentle"[26]
is a quote that penetrated my soul, made me feel something mental

somewhat of a realisation
that every calm and storm have their destination

like a phoenix born from the ashes
a thing of beauty created after enduring all its thrashes

they say a diamond is created under pressure
and a rainbow only presents itself after severe weather

so is it not plausible to accept
that you can and should expect

that whilst awful and shameful were the things you went through
that those will not be the cause of what breaks you, rather makes you

there is the potential in you to choose the monster
to blame your past for what breaks out and becomes a fraudster

but do you let the pain become you or use it to fuel a choice
two paths, one taken, to which is often and wrongly rejoiced

whilst the other less so
for it entails a hard-earned pro

---

[26]Anonymous

141

the one where you take your pain
roll it up into life experience and make it your gain

the one where you choose understanding
where you don't allow the violence to create your rebranding

rather the one where the unfortunate experience
becomes your fortune, invested in your serious

outlook on life, understanding that true strength is found in the gentle
because the world needs more people who are less judgemental

to choose violence is easy, to give in to the rage
whilst empathy comes from a wise man's wage

VICTOR

talking about your story doesn't make you a 'victim'
in fact, spreading awareness is what helps create a system

where people don't have to sit and be silent
as if talking about a wrong is some sort of indictment

as if sitting in silence makes you the better person all along
whilst talking about what happened apparently puts you in the wrong

but i beg to differ
because silence is conducive to something much stiffer

an environment of stillness
a lack of progression - illness

isn't that why we're all talking about mental health now
because we've finally learnt, a little late, about the power of speech now

you see validating our feelings
is what i call self-healing

so stop fostering a culture that encourages believing
that standing up for yourself makes your intentions deceiving

because if only we knew the amount of people we could have saved
if it weren't for this culture of silencing the pleas of those enslaved

told, "you've made your bed now lie in it"
even if someone makes them die in it

because god forbid someone's story should be heard
at the expense of damaging a family's reputation in turn

so instead we sentence these people to a life of cries unheard
because apparently that's better than to protect those who hurt

that way no one has to worry about the 'shame' that might bring
only they're forgetting about the pain that might sing

from their daughters, sons, sisters, brothers
who they're trying to silence for the satisfaction of others

if i had a dollar for every time someone said, "she's still your mother"
i'd be a millionaire by now but instead i discover

what happens when you help someone who has been abused
give them the space to talk about how they were used

encourage them to learn about how they can overcome
the terrible cards life dealt them and instead create a sum

of a life full of new memories
where one day they can stand in their own legacies

because they were let use their voice
a power not removed from their choice

and they were given the time to heal
from everything they had to ordeal

to talk about it, express themselves
despite the people implying that sharing one's story shames themselves

as if it's not the person committing the act
is the one who should be ashamed in fact

but those ignorant people aside
there are always others ready to listen inside

and i hope one day we all find our voice of power
used not only for ourselves but also for others, to empower

to help one heal from the pain caused by their inflictor
where they survive as not just a victim but also the victor

B.K

MY RENAISSANCE

8am in the morning
one eye open, yawning

my first thought being, "was it all dream"
or am i truly free to finally scream

not in anger but in relief
because younger me would be in disbelief

that i've woken up in a safe bed
you see it's the morning after i was offered refuge from my dread

the morning after i ran away from 'home'
the morning after i realised i was now finally home

free from all those pain filled years
having spent night after night drowning in tears

for twenty-two years i could never sleep in peace
because of the rent on my mental health and i was paying the lease

but not anymore, not from today
because yesterday my father helped me run away

to my blessing in disguise
to my other family, my prize

146

i listen closely, i hear my grandparents up and about
walking around, giggling through their snout

what a refreshing sound to hear
like a holiday in nature, waking up to birds cheer

i think i can accept now that this is all real
i can get up and finally start to heal

so one foot out from under the blanket
my heart is racing as if there was poison and i drank it

two feet out and on the ground
it's time to get up; i can hear a kettle's sound

now i know this isn't a dream for sure
because back where i'm from, i was the only one to do that 'chore'

i walk out into the kitchen to see grandad hand me a cup of tea
i'll never forget that, as silly as it sounds, no one has ever done that for me

perhaps that's what started this life-long obsession
of having a cup of tea before any and every session

as if it will always represent the start of a new day
both literally and figuratively, in each and every way

sipping that first taste of freedom
afforded to me that day, bequeathed them

that morning after i was given my rebirth
a chance to start over, begin again and reverse

slowly but surely, healing all the scars
paving my own path free from those bars

i sat down at the table and had my cup of tea
granny, grandad and i, just us three

we spent hours talking about everything that had happened
and then years patching up everything that had saddened

my entire childhood
but they promised that would not be the case for my adulthood

and i am grateful to report
that nine years later there has been nothing of the sort

so i want to take this opportunity to tell you all it gets better
there was a time i tried to throw in the towel forever

but i'm so glad i didn't
because if i had admitted

defeat and let that mother win
i would have robbed my life of all the beauty within

of the wholesome beauty from a real family
from people who genuinely love me, happily

of that morning after
where i finally got to begin a new chapter

where i wrote my own book, collected my own stories
travelled around the world and witnessed all its glories

now remember, no one's path is ever the same
the journey to recovery is indeed a pain

in truth, every struggle differs from one to the next
to put it simply, everyone's journey is complex

but i hope that in sharing with you my own story
you realise that everyone can work at their own journey

to your own morning after
your own new chapter

rewriting the story in the direction of your choice
until one day you close the book and can reflect and rejoice

for the life you led upon your rebirth
becoming your own parent on this earth

they say you can always reinvent yourself
so i guess that's what this is, a second chance for myself

this, this is my and can be your renaissance[27]
it's amazing what we can do with time, avec un peu de chance[28]

---

[27]A French word meaning "rebirth".
[28]French words meaning "with a bit of luck".

149

the dark is an ironic reminder that darkness never lasts

the sun always comes up in the morning, leaving it in our pasts

sincerely,

tomorrow

150

A NOTE FROM THE AUTHOR

THANK YOU

To anyone who has at all been a part of this journey of healing, be it in my real life or even in my online life, thank you. I want to take this moment to share with you all in writing, my deepest and most grateful of thank yous. It sounds cliché I'm sure but in truth a lot of things that are considered to be cliché (overused), perhaps are so for a reason; it is most fitting. Thus, it would be ignorant of me to not take the time to acknowledge, despite all my love for my references to my own sense of self-love and growth as an individual, to not also take the time to share my love intentionally, for all those who made this turn around in my life possible.

After running away from my mother, I spent years building the courage to share my story and eventually did so in the hopes that I may have the potential to be helping someone else out there, through their journey. I could not have done what I've done, if not for the blessing it was and still is, to have had somewhere to run to. Often when I make content in any capacity, where I reflect on when and why I ran away from home and the subsequent hard times that it resulted in (where I had to struggle with my mental health), I remind myself that at least I had a loving father to run to, despite the lack of a genuine mother. I know not everyone has that luxury and it is not, nor will it ever be, lost on me that I get to speak from such a context.

So first and foremost, I again want to thank the incredible family that took me back, healed me and saved me. I cannot stress enough how much they truly did save my life. Second, I want to say thank you to my online family, the audience that gave me a voice. I'm crying typing this to be honest and I think it's because I cannot express enough through words, what it's like having grown up in an environment where your voice was

B.K

silenced, where you weren't heard and yet now have so many of you that want to listen. You all are the reason I found strength, despite the inherent vulnerability, in attempting to be a part of the community that raises awareness for victims of child abuse.

My father's family have given me my life back but it was definitely my online family that gave me my voice back. The community we have built together is one that gave an abhorrent set of circumstances a sense of purpose, a reason to turn one's own victimhood into their own victorhood. Realising that you're not alone is perhaps one of the most therapeutic realisations in one's healing journey. To realise that, most unfortunately, there is a community out there that not only has had to endure similar circumstances to your own but that you can also heal with (therefore as a result build each other up and support each other's healing with), is something that fostered the foundations for some of the most peace I have ever attained over these last nine years.

I wish I could say this in every language that you all spoke but for now, thank you very much, go raibh míle maith agat and shukran jiddan. Here's to a life devoted to the recovery of all victims, into their era as their own victor, be that through poetry and/or any other helpful means.

In summary, thank you for being here and thank you for reading my book. May this book be a stepping stone for you as a part of your journey where you work towards the happiest and healthiest of futures. I hope that every time you return to this book, should you do so, you return that bit stronger, that bit more content and that bit more at peace.

As always, much love and God bless.
Berna xxx

Made in the USA
Monee, IL
30 January 2024

52327411R00085